IT'S METAL

If you look around, you will see lots of things made from metal. There are many different types of metal, and this book will show you what they are used for. We obtain metals like iron, gold and copper from under the ground. We can then use them for practical objects like bridges, or valuable things like jewellery. Gold is a very precious metal. It is rare and beautiful. Steel is very hard, and used for large, strong structures. In this book, you will learn all about these and many other uses of metal in the world today.

Each metal has its own special colour.
Some metals are shiny and hard.
They can be made into many
beautiful and useful things.

A MATERIAL WORLD

It's METAL

KAY DAVIES and WENDY OLDFIELD

WAYLAND

A MATERIAL WORLD

It's Glass It's Plastic
It's Metal It's Wood

Editor: Joanna Housley
Designer: Loraine Hayes

First published in 1992 by Wayland (Publishers) Ltd

This edition published in 2006 by Wayland, an imprint of Hachette Children's Books

British Library Cataloguing in Publication Data
Davies, Kay
It's Metal. – (A Material world)
I. Title II. Oldfield, Wendy III. Series
669

ISBN-10: 0750248491
ISBN-13: 9780750248495

Typeset by Kalligraphic Design Ltd, Horley, Surrey
Printed in China

Hachette Children's Books
338 Euston Road, London NW1 3BH

Words that appear in **bold** in the text are explained in the glossary on page 22.

Aluminium cans keep drinks fresh and fizzy. When they are empty we drop them in the bin.

They can be **recycled** to make new objects from the metal.

You may have seen some of these kitchen tools. They are made from metal because it can be strong and sharp. Do you know what the tools are used for?

Can you see all the metal dishes in this restaurant kitchen?

We use metal pots and pans for cooking because they heat up quickly and help cook our food.

The sharp edges of scissors help us cut carefully.

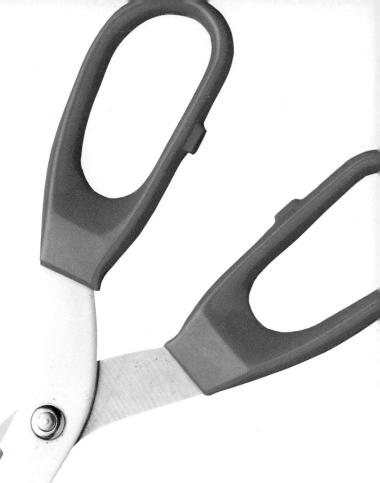

The handles help to make them safe and easy to use.

Magnets are made of iron and steel. They pull some metals towards them. How many paperclips are hanging from this magnet?

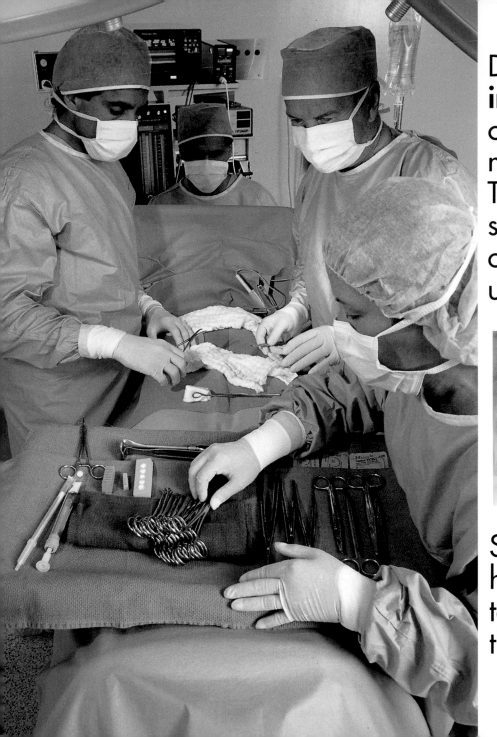

Doctors use metal **instruments** in operations to make people better. Their smooth surfaces can be cleaned and used again.

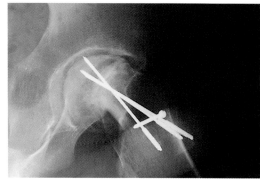

Strong metal pins hold broken bones together while they mend.

The weight-lifter pushes heavy metal weights high into the air.

He practises hard and tries to lift more weights each time.

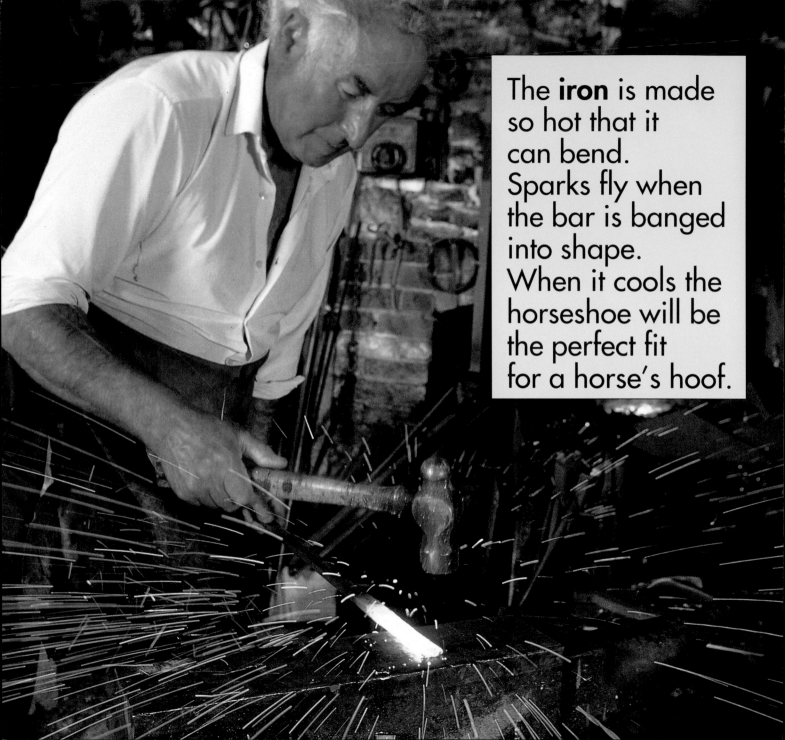

The **iron** is made so hot that it can bend. Sparks fly when the bar is banged into shape. When it cools the horseshoe will be the perfect fit for a horse's hoof.

Each little piece in a clock fits in with the others like a jigsaw. The **cogs** move round together to turn the hands of the clock.

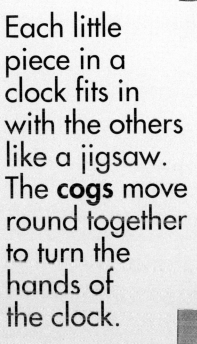

13

The boy can bounce and spin and do clever tricks on his bicycle.

The wheels and the hollow tubes of metal in the frame are strong enough to take his weight.

The train has a smooth shape to help it go fast.

It carries passengers safely over long distances. Its wheels follow metal tracks as it speeds along.

This musical instrument is a saxophone. It is made from a metal called brass.

The man can make music when he blows through it. We can listen or dance to its music.

Gold is a rare and valuable metal that lasts for ever. These golden domes glitter in the sunshine. They make an important place look very beautiful.

Steel bridges carry traffic over rivers.

The wind blowing through the metal **girders** cannot push the bridges down.

It is exciting to find old metal objects in the soil.

Thousands of years ago this **bronze shield** protected someone in battle.

The old car looks sad and worn. Once its paint shone and it worked well.

Now its iron body is **rusting** in the air and rain.

Scrap metal is piled high in the yard.
It will be melted down and new
things made from the old junk.

GLOSSARY

Aluminium A hard, light, silvery-white metal.

Bronze A brownish metal made from copper and tin.

Cogs Wheels with teeth on their edges. They fit and turn together.

Girders Steel beams used to hold up heavy loads.

Instrument A tool, such as a knife used by a doctor, or an object that can be played to produce musical sounds.

Iron A silvery-white, shiny metal.

Recycled Made into something new instead of being thrown away.

Rusting The effect of air and rain on iron which weakens it and wears it away.

Shield A piece of armour to protect the body.

Steel A hard, strong and long-lasting metal made from iron.

BOOKS TO READ

Ways into Science: Materials/Changing Materials by Peter Riley (Franklin Watts, 2001)

Working with Materials: Joining Materials/ Changing Materials/ Shaping Materials/ Mixing and Separating Materials by Chris Oxlade (Wayland, 2006)

TOPIC WEB

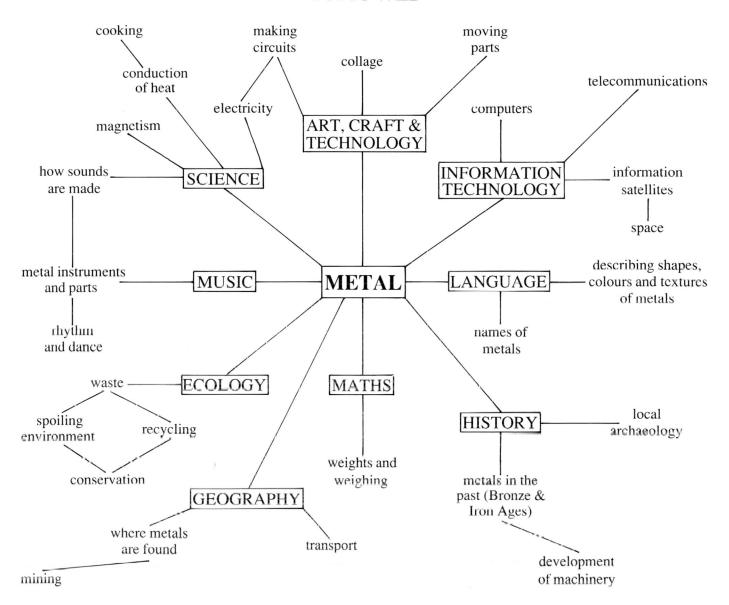

INDEX

aluminium 5

bicycle 14
bridges 18
bronze 19

cans 5
clock 13
cooking 7

gold 17

iron 12

recycling 5, 21
rust 20

scissors 8
steel 18

train 15

weights 11

Picture acknowledgements

Chapel Studios 8 (inset), 13; Eye Ubiquitous cover (top, Paul Seheult), 6 (Paul Seheult), 8 (main pic, Paul Seheult), 18 (Judyth Platt), 20 (Geoff Redmayne), 21 (Dave Fobister); St Mary's Hospital 10 (inset); Tony Stone Worldwide cover (left), 4, 10 (main pic), 12 (Rob Talbot), 14, 17 (Douglas Armand); Wayland Picture Library 7 (Michael Dent), 9 (Zul Mukhida), 15, 19 (British Museum); ZEFA 5, 11, 16.